5

In Georgian times music was very popular. New musical instruments were invented, including the violin, the cello and the piano. Most wealthy people had a piano in their home and they enjoyed playing music and singing.

Roger Coote and Diana Bentley

The Victorians and Georgians

Firefly

The Georgian age began almost 300 years ago in 1714. In that year George I became king of Britain. At that time many of the countries of Europe were ruled by kings and queens. They lived in huge royal palaces and had lots of servants to work for them. They gave their nobles important jobs in helping them to govern their countries.

In Britain, Holland and France companies were set up to **trade** with India and other countries in the East. They raised money from **investors** to pay for each voyage. When the ship returned the investors shared out the **profits** between them. Some of them became very rich.

The most famous trading company was the British East India Company. It was very powerful in India, and even had its own army.

Unlike many other countries in Europe, Britain was not ruled only by the king and his nobles. George I could not pass any laws unless they were agreed by **Parliament**. The men who met in the Houses of Parliament to discuss the laws represented the ordinary British people.

Although George I was the British king he was born in Germany and could not speak English. He left the running of the country to a group of 'ministers'. They were led by Robert Walpole, the Prime Minister.

The Georgian age was a time of new ideas. In France, a group of men called 'philosophers' said that all people had rights which could not be taken away from them. They believed that people were equal and that one group of people should not rule over the rest. Their **democratic** ideas were not very popular with the rulers of Europe.

Many British people had sailed across the Atlantic to set up **colonies** in America. They went to start a new life in a new land. But they still had to depend on Britain. They paid British taxes but they were too far away to play a part in government.

In 1776 they announced that they wanted to govern themselves instead of being ruled by Britain. The two sides fought a war and the Americans won. They founded the United States of America and based their government on the ideas of democracy.

15

In Georgian times travel was difficult and expensive. People in the countryside were often cut off from the towns. So they made their own entertainment. Sometimes they gathered in the fields to sing and dance in the open air. The game of cricket also became very popular in country villages.

During the time of the Georgians science advanced rapidly. One of the most exciting inventions was first seen in France. It was the hot-air balloon built by the Montgolfier brothers.

An important discovery was electricity. Can you imagine what life would be like without it?

19

A **revolution** began in France in 1789. The people in Paris and other French cities fought for their democratic rights – '**liberty, equality** and **fraternity**'. They defeated the king and his nobles and formed their own government. The revolution was very violent and thousands of people were killed, including the king and queen of France.

In 1837 Queen Victoria came to the British throne and the Victorian age began. During this period many great changes took place. Railway lines were built to all parts of the country. People who lived in small towns and villages were able to travel and visit their friends and relatives. They travelled in trains pulled by steam engines.

23

Steam engines were also used to power machines in new **factories**. Many of the factories made cloth from cotton. Cotton was grown on **plantations** in the United States. When the crop was ready it had to be harvested quickly in case a storm damaged it. Many of the people who worked in the cotton fields were **slaves** who had been taken from Africa to work for the rich plantation owners. Their lives were very hard and they were often treated badly by their masters.

In Britain many people left the countryside to find work in the towns. Men, women and even children worked for long hours in noisy, dangerous factories. They made cloth, iron, pottery, glass, soap and many other things. The factory machines were often powered by burning coal, and tall chimneys poured thick, black smoke into the air.

27

Victorian scientists and inventors made many new machines. Some of them were for use in factories, and others were for people to use at home. The **gramophone** was an early type of record-player. For the first time people could listen to recorded music and words. The sound came out of a large horn.

The Victorian age ended in 1901 when Queen Victoria died. It had brought a great many changes in science, industry and transport, and in the way people lived.

New words

Colonies   Groups of people who move from one country to live in another country.

Democratic   A situation in which all people have equal rights and are free to choose who governs them.

Factories   Buildings in which goods are made, often using machines.

Fraternity   When a group of people have the same interests and wishes.

Gramophone   An old name for a record-player. The first gramophone records were shaped like round tubes rather than flat discs.

Investors   People who put up money for a business. They hope to get their money back and make some more money too if the business is a success.

Liberty   The freedom to act as you want.

Parliament   The group of people who govern Britain.

Plantation   A very large farm where crops are grown to be sold in other countries.

Profits   When investors put up money for a business they hope to get back more money than they spent. The extra amount they get is called profit.

Revolution   A great change which takes place quite quickly.

Slaves   People who belong to another person and are forced to work for them.

Trade   Buying and selling goods for money or swapping them for other goods.

Books to read

If you would like to find out more about the people who lived in Georgian and Victorian times, these books will help you.

Everyday Life in the Eighteenth Century by Neil Grant (Macdonald)
Walpole and the Georgians by S. Hopewell (Wayland)
Growing Up in Victorian England by Molly Harrison (Wayland)
Everyday Life in the Nineteenth Century by Neil Grant (Macdonald)
How They Lived – A Victorian Factory Worker by Stewart Ross (Wayland)
The Victorians by Miriam Moss (Wayland)
Queen Victoria by Dorothy Turner (Wayland)